INSPIRING KURDISH WOMEN

Written by **Ruwayda Mustafah**
Illustrated by **Miftahuljannah Siregar**

Inspiring Kurdish Women

Written by Ruwayda Mustafah
Illustrated by Miftahuljannah Siregar

Copyright © 2022 Ruwayda Mustafah

All rights reserved. No part of this book may be reproduced or used in any manner without the prior written permission of the copyright owner, except for the use of brief quotations in a book review.

ISBN: 9798433385757

This book belongs to

....

Lady Adela Jaff

1847-1924

In the fascinating world of Kurdish history, there lived a remarkable woman named Lady Adela Jaff. Born into the esteemed Sahibqeran family, her story intertwined with her marriage to Osman Pasha Jaff, the revered Kurdish King of the Jaff tribe. Together, they embarked on an extraordinary journey that would change the lands they governed forever.

While her husband fulfilled his duties as the leader of the Jaff tribe, Lady Adela emerged as a shining example of strength and leadership. She fearlessly defied the expectations of society and took charge. Under her wise rule, a small village bloomed into a lively town. Even the once barren lands transformed into fertile fields, bursting with life and abundance.

In the absence of her husband, Lady Adela showcased exceptional wisdom in establishing law and order. Guided by a strong sense of justice, she oversaw the construction of a prison, ensuring peace and harmony among her people. To make sure everyone's voice was heard, she created a court of justice where disputes were settled fairly and grievances were given careful consideration.

Lady Adela's courage and determination made her famous far beyond the borders of Kurdistan. Her bravery inspired all who heard her remarkable story. During the turbulent times of World War I, she showed great compassion to British soldiers, offering them refuge and solace amidst the chaos of battle. Her incredible acts of courage earned her the well-deserved title of the "princess of the brave," a testament to her unwavering spirit and selflessness.

But Lady Adela's quest for justice didn't stop there. In a time when the idea of women's rights was hotly debated, she became a true pioneer. Lady Adela Jaff's name will forever be remembered in the pages of history. She was a visionary leader, a compassionate refuge, and an unwavering champion of justice and equality. Her remarkable contributions to her people solidify her rightful place among the esteemed figures of Kurdish history, leaving an enduring legacy for generations to come.

Mastureh Ardalan
1805-1848

Mastureh Ardalan, a Kurdish poet, historian, and writer, embarked on a remarkable journey that defied societal norms and paved the way for women's education and empowerment. Despite living in a time when women were not allowed to study, she became the first-published historian in Iran, leaving an indelible mark on history.

Through her written works, Mastureh Ardalan delved into the realms of poetry, history, and literature, crafting captivating stories that transported readers to different times and places. Her dedication and talent were unparalleled, setting her apart as a pioneer in her field. Notably, she held the distinction of being the sole female historiographer in the Middle East until the late nineteenth century.

Born into a prominent family, Mastureh Ardalan's journey was shaped by her remarkable achievements and her courage to challenge the status quo. Her trailblazing spirit inspired women, serving as a catalyst for their fight for suffrage and equal rights. In recognition of her monumental contributions, a monument was created in the Kurdistan Region to honour her legacy and commemorate her lasting impact.

Even today, Mastureh Ardalan's legacy continues to resonate, inspiring women and girls across all parts of Kurdistan. Her story serves as a reminder that determination and perseverance can overcome barriers, and that one individual's actions can shape the course of history.

Mastureh Ardalan's name stands as a testament to the power of education, the pursuit of knowledge, and the unwavering spirit that can change the world. Her story inspires us to dream big, embrace our potential, and strive for progress and equality in all aspects of life.

Hapsa Khan
1881-1953

Hapsa Khan, an influential figure in the early Kurdish feminist movement, dedicated her life to championing women's right to education. Born into the esteemed family of Sheikh Marif and Salma Khan, Hapsa embarked on a transformative journey that would leave a lasting impact on the lives of Kurdish women.

With unwavering determination, Hapsa established the first school in Iraq specifically for women, known as the Kurdish Women's Association. She tirelessly advocated for education, traversing her local community and persuading parents to embrace the idea of sending their daughters to her school.

Beyond her passion for education, Hapsa had a deep love for travel and photography. She captured the beauty of the world through her camera lens, and her wanderlust inspired her to explore new horizons. Additionally, she found joy in collecting stamps, amassing a remarkable album that contained 677 stamps from various countries.

Upon her passing in 1953, Hapsa Khan's home underwent a remarkable transformation. It was repurposed into a school, serving as a poignant reminder of her unwavering dedication to education and her enduring legacy.

Hapsa Khan's story serves as a testament to the power of education and the pursuit of equality. Her efforts paved the way for countless Kurdish women to access education, empowering them to shape their own destinies. Her love for exploration and collecting stamps reminds us to embrace our passions and find joy in the world around us.

Today, Hapsa Khan's memory lives on as an inspiration to all, encouraging us to strive for knowledge, equality, and the pursuit of our dreams. Her impact continues to shape the lives of generations, leaving an indelible mark on the path towards a more inclusive and empowered society.

Leila Bedir Khan
1903-1986

Leila Bedir Khan, born into a noble household, was surrounded by a rich cultural heritage. Her father, Abdurezzak Bedir Khan, served as a diplomat in the Ottoman Empire, while her mother, Henriette Ornik, was a talented dentist with Austrian Jewish roots.

Leila's passion for dance took her on an extraordinary journey across Europe and the United States. She mesmerized audiences with her captivating performances, showcasing her unique solo choreographies that often incorporated traditional Kurdish dances. In a moment of pride, she proclaimed, "I am the first Kurd to dance at La Scala," referring to the renowned Opera House in Milan, Italy.

Leila's path as a dancer was not without challenges. In a time when society frowned upon women pursuing dance or performing in public, she fearlessly defied societal norms. Her creative expression shattered stereotypes, and her debut performance garnered attention from prestigious publications like the New York Times, which affectionately dubbed her the "Kurdistan princess."

Leila Bedir Khan's legacy goes beyond her remarkable talent as a dancer. She symbolizes the power of breaking barriers and embracing one's true passions, regardless of societal expectations. Through her artistry, she challenged gender stereotypes and paved the way for future generations of female performers.

Leila's story serves as an inspiration to all, reminding us to fearlessly pursue our dreams and celebrate our unique cultural heritage. Her contributions to the world of dance and her courage in challenging societal norms will forever be remembered, solidifying her place as a trailblazer in the realm of performing arts.

LEYLA ZANA

Leyla Zana, a Kurdish politician, has left an indelible mark on history. Born in Amed, she made history as the first Kurdish woman elected to the Turkish Parliament. Her courageous actions and unwavering dedication to her people have garnered international recognition, including the prestigious Sakharov Prize awarded by the European Parliament in 1995.

In 1991, Leyla Zana created a stir when she boldly spoke in the Kurdish language within Turkey's parliament. Her act of embracing her cultural identity sparked controversy and highlighted the struggle for linguistic and cultural rights. Shockingly, she was sentenced to 15 years in prison simply for expressing herself in her native language. Amnesty International swiftly declared her a prisoner of conscience, shining a spotlight on the injustice she faced.

Leyla Zana's unwavering commitment to peace and justice has earned her two Nobel Peace Prize nominations. Even after her release from prison, she remained steadfast in her pursuit of a peaceful resolution to the Kurdish question in Turkey. Through her advocacy and tireless work, she continues to champion the rights of her people and strive for a harmonious future.

Leyla Zana's story serves as a powerful reminder of the importance of standing up for one's beliefs, even in the face of adversity. Her resilience and determination inspire others to fight for justice and equality. She has become a symbol of hope and a beacon of change, not only for the Kurdish community but for people around the world who strive for peace and human rights.

Leyla Zana's legacy will forever be intertwined with the ongoing struggle for Kurdish rights and the pursuit of a peaceful resolution. Her unwavering spirit and dedication to justice serve as a guiding light for future generations, reminding us all of the power of one individual's voice in shaping a brighter tomorrow.

Lenya Run

Lenya Rún, a politician of Kurdish heritage in Iceland, is a rising force in the political landscape. In 2021, she came close to becoming the country's youngest member of parliament, although she ultimately lost her seat due to a reshuffle. Currently serving as a deputy member of parliament, she is also a final-year law student, showcasing her commitment to both education and public service.

As an advocate for change, Lenya Rún focuses on improving the rights of asylum seekers and addressing the pressing issue of climate change. Her dedication to these crucial causes reflects her deep sense of responsibility and empathy for those in need. Growing up with parents from the Kurdistan region, she holds her heritage dear, and she aspires to promote inclusivity and equitable representation for all minorities through her political career.

Lenya Rún's determination to make a difference is an inspiration to young people everywhere. Despite setbacks, she remains steadfast in her pursuit of positive societal change. By advocating for the rights of asylum seekers and working towards solutions for the climate crisis, she actively contributes to building a more compassionate and sustainable future.

With her passion, intelligence, and commitment, Lenya Rún embodies the potential for young leaders to effect meaningful change. Her journey serves as a reminder that age is not a barrier to making a difference and that even small actions can have a significant impact on society. As she continues to develop her political career, she will undoubtedly play a vital role in shaping Iceland's future and beyond.

SOZA MOHAMED

Soza Mohamed, a prominent lifestyle blogger and influencer hailing from Sulaymaniyah, captivates audiences with her inspiring journey. Recognized as one of the 100 influential women in the Kurdistan region, her impact extends far beyond her online presence.

By day, Soza shares her passion for the English language as a college instructor, showcasing her dedication to education. But her talents don't stop there—she is a multifaceted young woman with a flair for creativity. Soza's poetic expressions and captivating skills as a Daf player make her a true artistic force.

Harnessing the power of social media, Soza fearlessly challenges stereotypes about women. Through her engaging content and active participation in workshops and panel discussions, she empowers others to break free from societal expectations. With a strong belief in self-acceptance and body positivity, she encourages individuals to embrace their unique qualities and celebrate their authentic selves.

Soza Mohamed's impact extends beyond the virtual realm, as she inspires countless individuals to embrace their passions, express themselves, and challenge the status quo. Her dedication to education, artistic endeavors, and advocating for self-acceptance makes her a shining example of how one person's voice can create positive change. By encouraging others to love themselves and promoting inclusivity, Soza is helping to shape a more accepting and diverse society.

Lanja Khawe

Lanja Khawe, a dedicated lawyer and champion of human rights, hails from the vibrant city of Sulaymaniyah. With a fierce focus on women's rights, she has become a true agent of change. As the founder of the Sofia Association, a remarkable non-profit organization, Lanja has transformed countless lives by offering shelter to the homeless and providing crucial legal and immediate support to the most vulnerable members of society.

Throughout her career, Lanja has tirelessly provided legal aid and advocated for women who have suffered from domestic violence. In 2016, she embarked on an inspiring campaign that involved distributing books on bicycles across Sulaymaniyah city, igniting a culture of reading and knowledge-sharing.

Beyond her hands-on work, Lanja continues to make a lasting impact on women's rights through policy advocacy. Her unwavering determination has driven her to challenge patriarchal barriers and encourage young women to actively engage in their communities. By fostering a sense of empowerment and community involvement, she is reshaping the landscape and breaking down societal barriers.

Lanja Khawe stands as a true inspiration, demonstrating the profound impact that one person can make in fighting for justice and equality. Her dedication to women's rights, her compassion for the vulnerable, and her commitment to empowering the next generation exemplify the transformative power of activism. Through her tireless efforts, Lanja is driving positive change and creating a more inclusive and equitable society for all.

Sayran Barzani

Sayran Barzani, an esteemed American Kurd and talented jewellery designer, has made her mark in the vibrant city of Los Angeles. In 2016, she boldly established her own label, aptly named Sayran, which showcases her exquisite creations. Her jewellery designs are deeply rooted in her Kurdish heritage, with the symbolic evil-eye emblem taking center stage, reflecting both protection and cultural significance.

Through her artistic craftsmanship, Sayran Barzani expresses her profound connection to her roots, using jewellery as a medium to honor her heritage. Not only does she create stunning pieces, but she also uses her talent to support charitable causes and initiatives. Sayran has been actively involved in fundraising efforts, using her jewellery to make a positive impact on various charitable organizations. Her commitment to giving back to the community is as beautiful as her creations themselves.

Sayran's jewellery collections are a vibrant tapestry of colors, reflecting the diversity and richness of cultures. Each piece tells a story and celebrates the strength that comes from embracing our differences. With her forward-thinking approach, Sayran has garnered well-deserved recognition and admiration. She is not only a designer but also an advocate for sustainable fashion practices. Embracing the urgency of climate change, Sayran promotes upcycling and champions the importance of sustainable fashion. Her innovative ideas and dedication to creating a more environmentally conscious industry have earned her acclaim and admiration.

Sayran Barzani's journey as a jewellery designer embodies the power of art to bridge cultures, express heritage, and promote positive change. Through her creations, she celebrates diversity, supports charitable endeavors, and advocates for sustainability. With each unique piece, Sayran weaves a story that inspires and uplifts, leaving an indelible mark on the world of jewellery design.

Dr. Raman Rashwany

Dr. Raman Rashwany is a trailblazing consultant liaison psychiatrist in the United Kingdom, breaking barriers and making a significant impact in the field of mental health. As the first Kurdish woman to become a member of the esteemed Royal College of Psychiatrists, she has paved the way for others to follow in her footsteps.

With her expertise and dedication, Dr. Rashwany plays a pivotal role in the mental health landscape, overseeing an impressive workload of 4,000 referrals each year. She brings her compassionate care and specialized knowledge to the largest department of liaison psychiatry in North West London, making a tangible difference in the lives of countless individuals.

Recognized for her invaluable contributions, Dr. Rashwany was celebrated as an unsung hero in psychiatry as part of the prestigious 25 Women project by the Royal College of Psychiatrists. This accolade highlights her unwavering commitment to mental health wellbeing and acknowledges her exceptional contributions to the field.

Beyond her professional achievements, Dr. Rashwany is an advocate for mental health awareness, tirelessly working to promote wellbeing and reduce stigma surrounding mental health issues. Her dedication to her patients and her advocacy for improved mental health services make her a true role model and a champion of change.

Dr. Raman Rashwany's remarkable journey as a Kurdish woman in psychiatry showcases the power of perseverance and the impact one individual can have in transforming lives. Her pioneering spirit, combined with her expertise and compassion, has made her a respected figure in the field, inspiring future generations of psychiatrists and bringing hope to those in need of mental health support.

Dr. Esrah Kamal Shah Mohammed

Dr. Esrah Kamal Shah Mohammed is a dedicated medical doctor and a passionate advocate for healthy living. With a master's degree in nutrition from King's College London, she combines her medical expertise and nutritional knowledge to inspire positive changes in people's lives.

Using the power of social media, Dr. Mohammed spreads awareness about the importance of healthy eating and a nutritious lifestyle. Through her engaging content, she aims to transform the way people perceive food and encourage them to make informed choices that benefit their overall well-being.

Dr. Mohammed is driven by a desire to reshape the way we approach health problems, particularly obesity and unhealthy habits. Her innovative approach focuses on finding practical solutions that individuals can easily incorporate into their lives, promoting long-term well-being and reducing the prevalence of these issues.

One of Dr. Mohammed's primary goals is to empower young children to develop healthy habits early on, ensuring they grow into strong, vibrant, and happy adults. By instilling the value of nutritious food and promoting positive relationships with food, she hopes to make a lasting impact on their overall health and well-being.

Dr. Esrah Kamal Shah Mohammed is a visionary advocate for change, striving to create a healthier society by transforming our relationship with food. Her dedication to helping individuals adopt healthier lifestyles and her commitment to promoting nutritious eating habits make her an influential figure in the field of nutrition and medicine. Through her work, she aspires to inspire people of all ages to embrace a nutritious lifestyle and enjoy the benefits of a balanced diet.

Taban Shoresh

Taban Shoresh is a remarkable aid worker, a survivor of the Anfal genocide, and the visionary founder of The Lotus Flower, a non-profit organization dedicated to supporting women affected by conflict in the Middle East.

With unwavering dedication, Taban strives to provide immediate assistance to displaced women who have experienced the devastating consequences of war. Her organization offers essential support, empowering these courageous women to rebuild their lives and reclaim their futures.

Taban is a passionate advocate for refugee women, recognizing the challenges they face in reintegrating into their communities. Through The Lotus Flower, she goes beyond providing aid and equips these resilient individuals with valuable skills, enabling them to seize new opportunities and pursue meaningful employment.

As a One Young World Ambassador, Taban has taken her advocacy to the global stage, inspiring audiences worldwide. Her powerful voice resonates at international events, where she passionately champions the empowerment of girls and women. Through her compelling speeches, she sheds light on the struggles and triumphs of refugee women, advocating for their rights and amplifying their voices.

Taban Shoresh's work is an embodiment of hope and resilience. Her dedication to supporting displaced women, empowering them with skills, and advocating for their rights has earned her admiration and respect. Through The Lotus Flower and her influential role as a global advocate, Taban continues to make a profound impact, transforming the lives of countless women and fostering a brighter future for all.

Raz Xaidan

Raz Xaidan is an extraordinary multidisciplinary artist who fearlessly explores the dynamic intersections of time, identity, and resistance through her captivating work. In 2014, she founded The Darling Beast, a brand that encompasses a virtual shop offering a range of artistic creations, including stickers, prints, and notebooks.

Recently, Raz Xaidan joined forces with The Lotus Flower organization, lending her artistic prowess to support a worthy cause. Through this partnership, she has helped cover the financial expenses of a short literacy course designed specifically for women survivors of conflict. By investing in their education, she empowers these resilient women to shape their own narratives and build a brighter future.

As the visionary founder of The Jiyan Archives, Raz Xaidan has created a powerful platform to document the lived experiences of Kurdish women from diverse backgrounds. Through her art, she sheds light on a unique and often overlooked part of Kurdish history, giving voice to the untold stories and celebrating the strength and resilience of Kurdish women.

Raz Xaidan's artistic expressions serve as a bridge between the past, present, and future, weaving together threads of identity and resistance. Her work challenges conventional narratives and invites viewers to delve deeper into the complexities of Kurdish heritage. With every stroke of her brush and every stroke of her pen, she unveils the rich tapestry of Kurdish history and amplifies the voices of those who have been marginalized.

Through her artistry and dedication, Raz Xaidan continues to be a beacon of inspiration, provoking thought and promoting dialogue. Her contributions to the artistic and cultural landscape not only honor the past but also pave the way for a more inclusive and diverse future.

Payzee Mahmod

Payee Mahmod is an incredible champion in the fight against child marriage and a dedicated advocate for women's rights within the United Kingdom. Having personally experienced the hardships of child marriage, she has emerged as a powerful voice against this harmful practice and played a pivotal role in successfully leading a campaign to ban it in the country.

Payee Mahmod's tireless efforts and unwavering commitment to ending child marriage have garnered widespread recognition. In 2021, she was honored as the UK Parliament Volunteer of the Year, a testament to her impactful advocacy work. Her dedication and achievements were also acknowledged at the UN Women UK Awards in 2020, highlighting her significant contributions to the advancement of women's rights.

Currently, Payee Mahmod works with the women's rights organization IKWRO, which provides crucial support and assistance to women from Middle Eastern, North African, and Afghan backgrounds. Through her involvement with IKWRO, she empowers and uplifts women, ensuring they have the resources and guidance needed to navigate and overcome the challenges they face.

As a vocal advocate for women's rights, Payee Mahmod is instrumental in raising awareness about the issues affecting marginalized communities. Her activism and determination serve as an inspiration to others, shining a light on the importance of equality and justice for all. By speaking out against child marriage and working towards a more inclusive society, she is making a profound impact and creating positive change for women and girls across the United Kingdom.

Tafan Hama

Tafan Hama is a remarkable entrepreneur and trailblazer in the field of cosmetics. As the founder of the successful Decorum Company and the cosmetic line By Taff, she has established herself as an expert in marketing, branding, and event management. Her extensive knowledge and passion for the beauty industry have propelled her to create a diverse range of products, including skincare, haircare, and fragrances, under the brand name By Taff.

What sets Tafan apart is not only her entrepreneurial spirit but also her role as a leading woman in Kurdistan's business landscape. In an industry traditionally dominated by men, Tafan has broken barriers and emerged as a shining example for aspiring female entrepreneurs. By fearlessly navigating uncharted territory, she has paved the way for other women to pursue their dreams and establish their own businesses.

Tafan's cosmetic line, By Taff, showcases her dedication to quality and innovation. Through meticulous research and a deep understanding of consumer preferences, she has created products that cater to a diverse range of needs and preferences. Her commitment to excellence has earned her a loyal customer base and positioned By Taff as a trusted brand within the beauty industry.

Beyond her entrepreneurial pursuits, Tafan Hama is actively involved in empowering other women. By sharing her experiences and insights, she inspires and encourages aspiring female entrepreneurs to believe in themselves and pursue their ambitions. Through her success, Tafan proves that with determination, resilience, and a strong vision, women can thrive and make their mark in any field they choose.

Rez Gardi

Rez Gardi is an exceptional individual who has dedicated her life to fighting for justice and empowering others. As an international lawyer and human rights activist, she has made significant contributions to the betterment of society. Her remarkable achievements have earned her widespread recognition, including being named Young New Zealander of the Year in 2017.

A true trailblazer, Rez shattered barriers by becoming the first Kurdish woman to graduate from Harvard Law School in 2019. Her commitment to human rights and her impressive academic achievements led her to receive the prestigious Harvard Satter Human Rights Fellowship, which recognized her outstanding work in Iraq.

Driven by her passion to make a difference, Rez founded EMPOWER, a dynamic youth-led organization that strives to increase the representation of refugees in higher education. Through EMPOWER, she offers vital support to young people by providing educational opportunities, fostering leadership skills, and promoting capacity building. By empowering youth, Rez aims to create a brighter future and break the cycle of inequality and marginalization.

Rez's impact extends beyond her educational initiatives. Her influential voice was recognized on a global scale when she was awarded the Outstanding Youth Delegate Award at the UN Youth Assembly in 2019. This prestigious honor further highlights her dedication and effectiveness in advocating for youth rights and amplifying their voices in international forums.

Rez Gardi's journey is a testament to the power of determination and the ability to effect change. Through her unwavering commitment to human rights, education, and youth empowerment, she has become a role model for aspiring activists and leaders around the world. Rez's tireless efforts and remarkable accomplishments inspire others to stand up for justice, embrace education as a transformative tool, and advocate for the rights and well-being of all individuals.

Printed in Great Britain
by Amazon